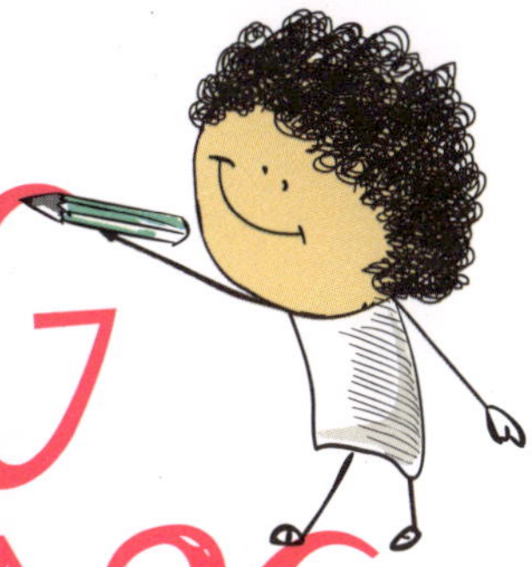

DRAWING & PAINTING TECHNIQUES

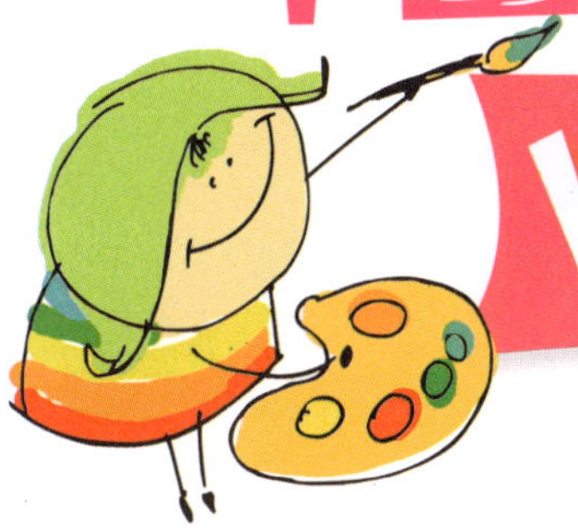

WORKBOOK

Level 4

AF516741

Om KIDZ
An imprint of Om Books International

Design Square

Use squares of different sizes to complete this design.

Colour the design using different shades of blue.

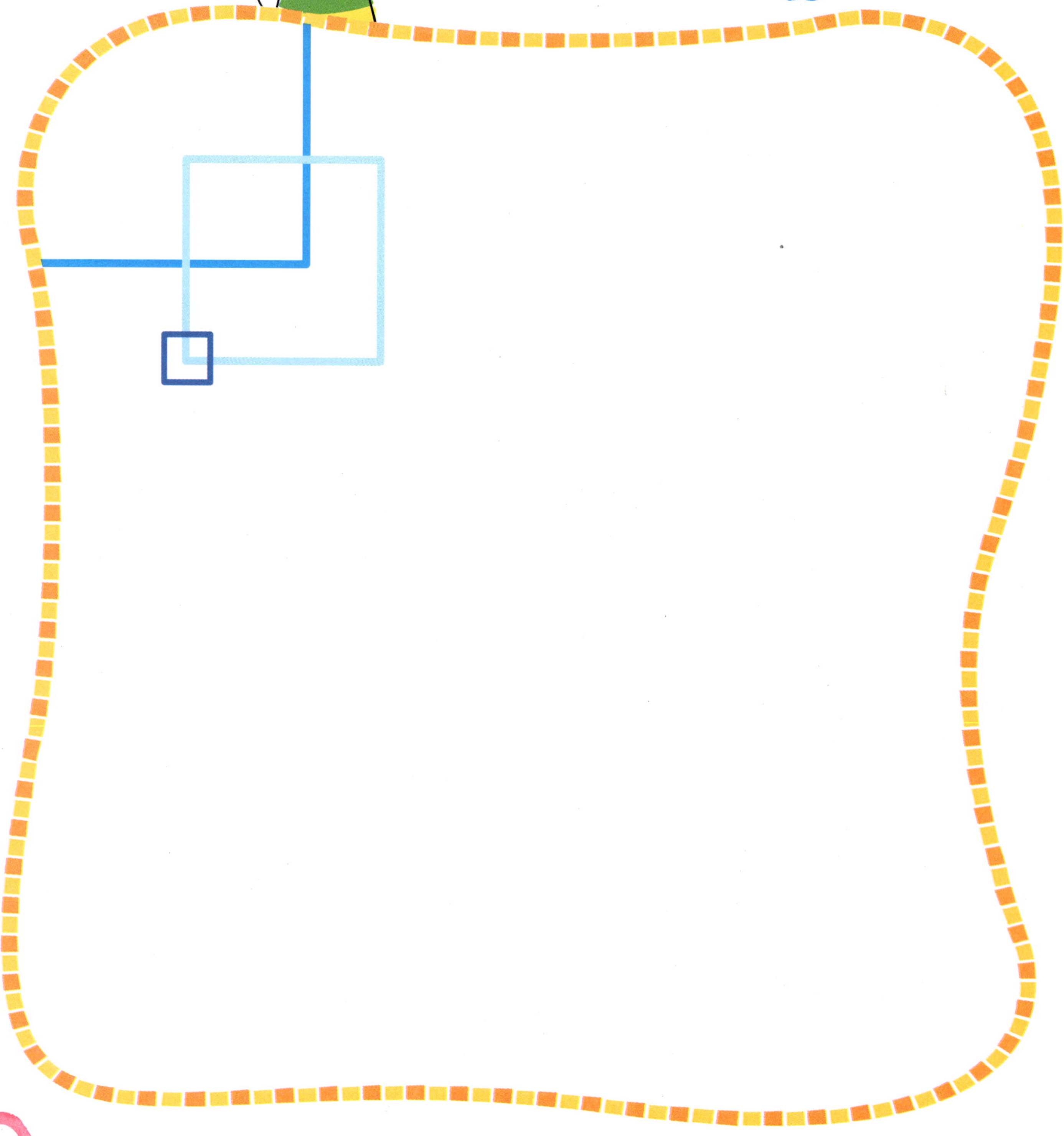

Fat Black Lines

Extend the fat black line to create a design so that each shape is connected by the line.

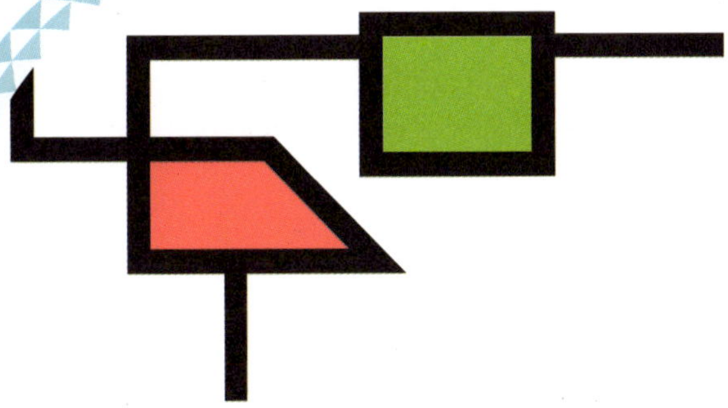

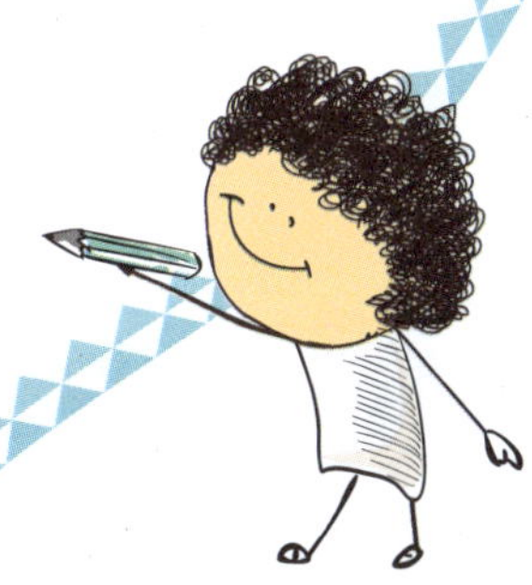

White space in a design is called negative space. It helps highlight the main design. The design is called positive space.

Fairy Lights

Cut out a sheet of paper in the shape of a light bulb. Place it below and colour the edges with coloured crayons. When you remove the paper, it will look like glowing lights.

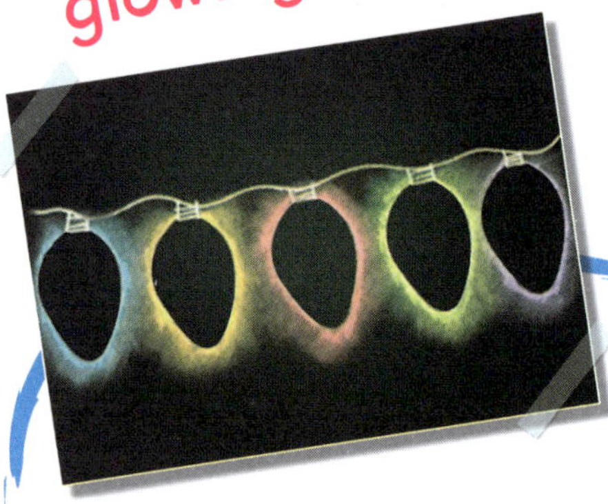

Spread the colour spread the crayon colour with a piece of paper when you place the light bulb below.

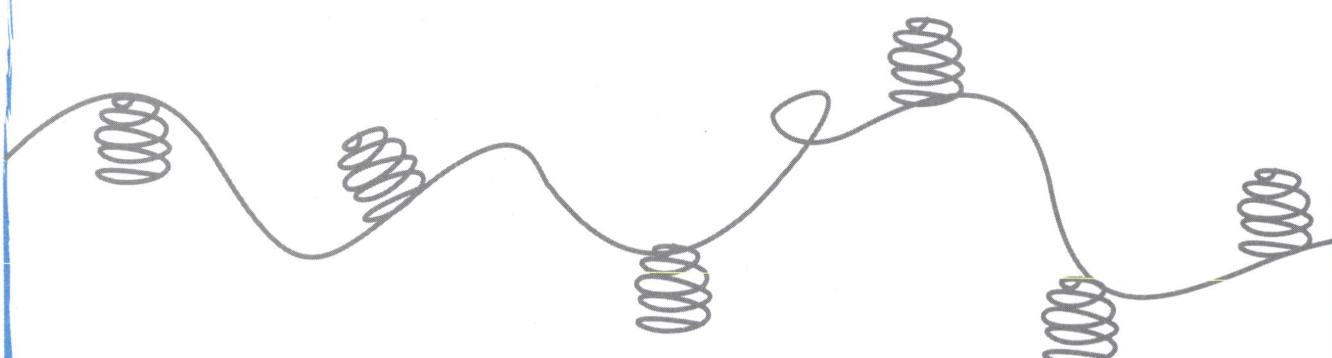

Draw a Castle

Use the elements given below to draw your own castle.

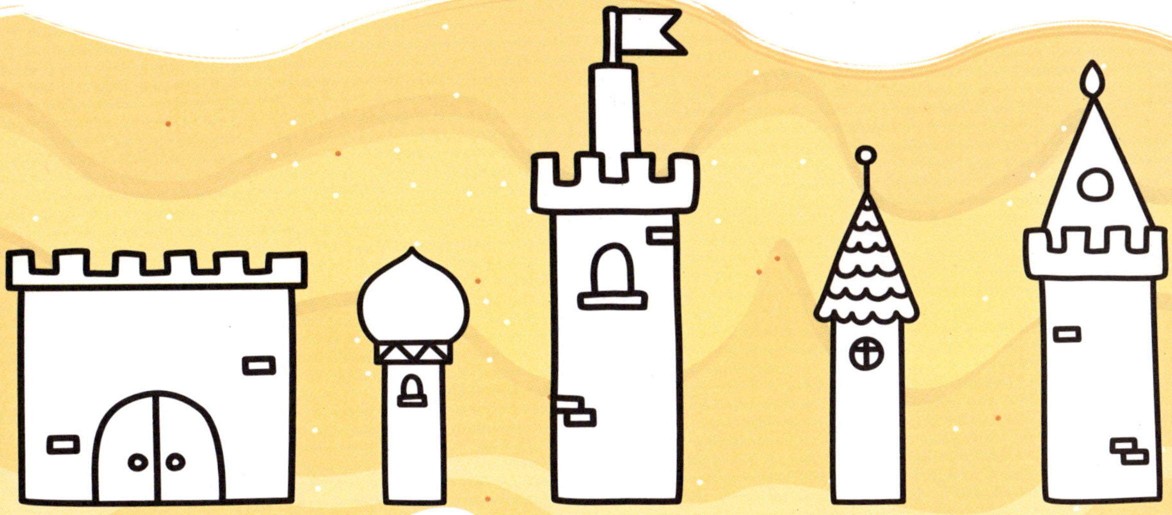

Fun Shading

Practice shading using different coloured pencils in the space given below.

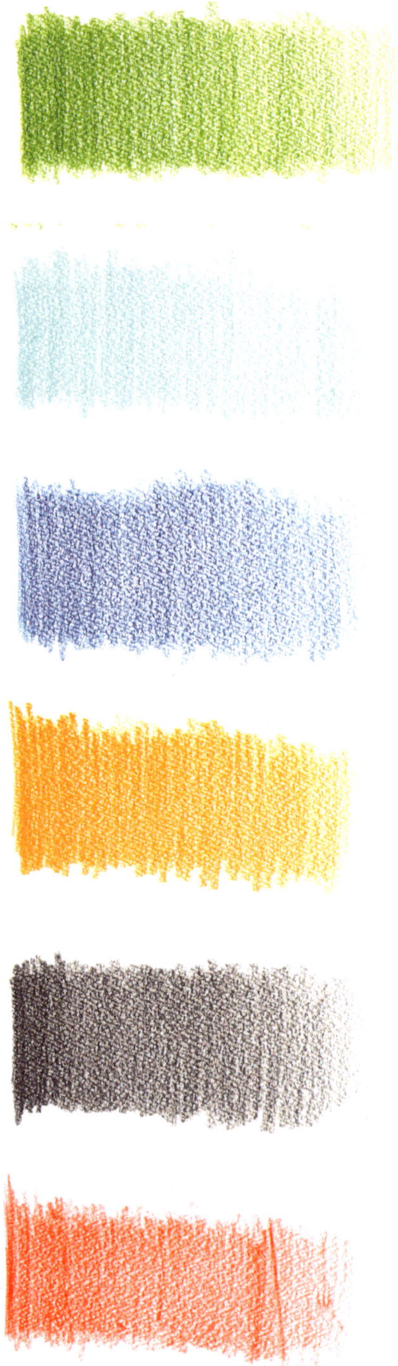

Draw a landscape and colour it using the shading technique you just learnt.

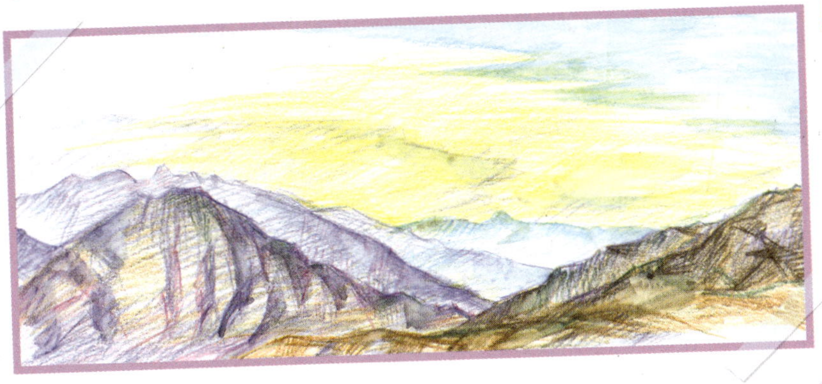

For darker areas, apply more pressure to the pencil. For lighter areas, apply less pressure to the pencil.

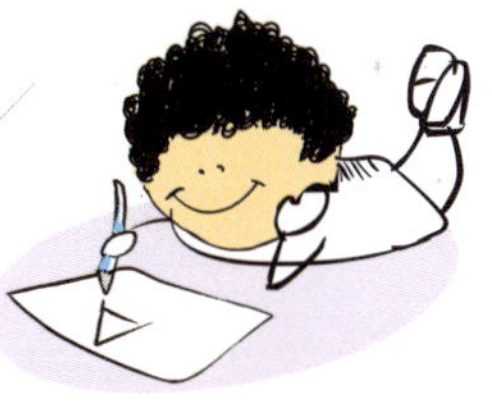

3D Fun

You can change flat shapes into three dimensional shapes by shading them properly. Try your hand at drawing and shading these three-dimensional shapes.

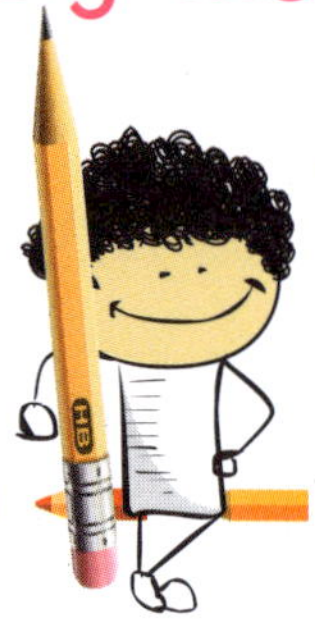

Use 2B, 4B and 6B pencils to shade these shapes.

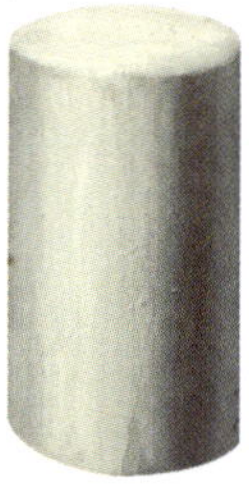

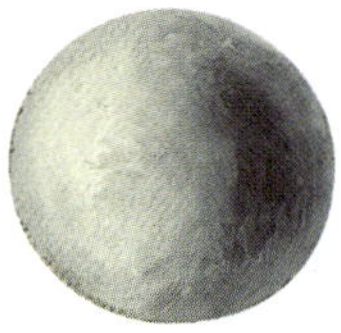

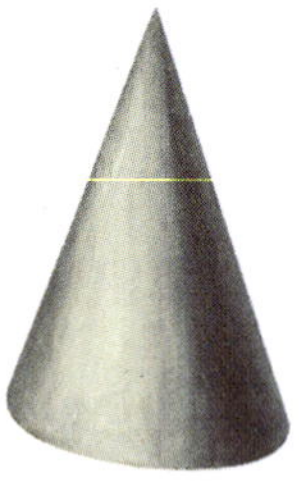

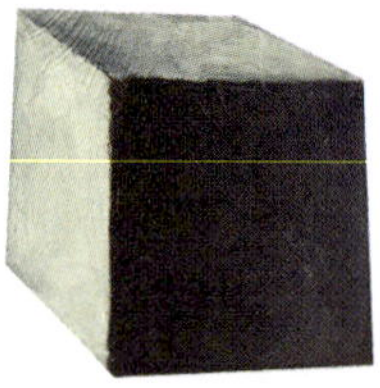

Black and White

Use pencils to draw this picture. Then, shade it with the help of pencils.

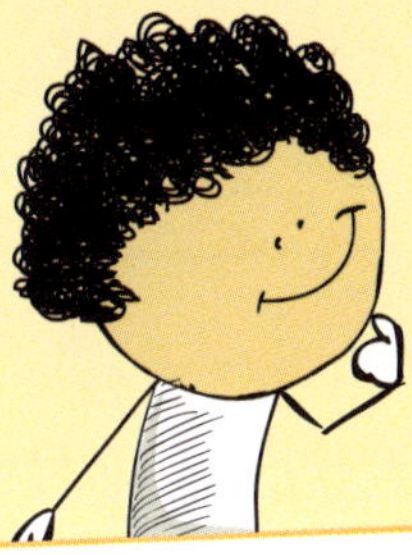

Begin where the shading has to be the lightest.

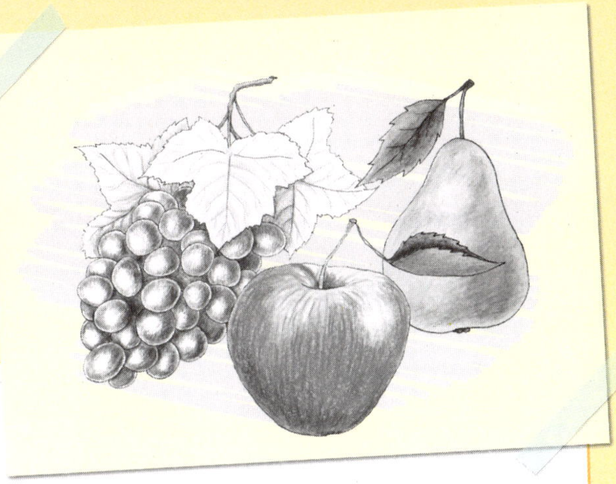

Van Gogh

Practice circular strokes with a little flat brush. Use the same technique to make a landscape in the space given below.

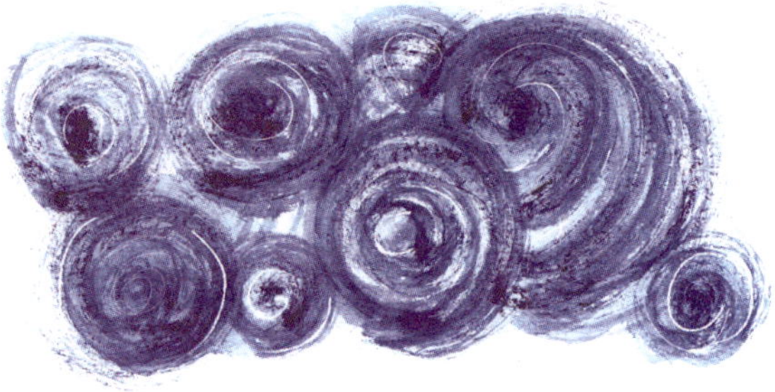

You just learnt the Van Gogh style of painting. Van Gogh was a famous painter.

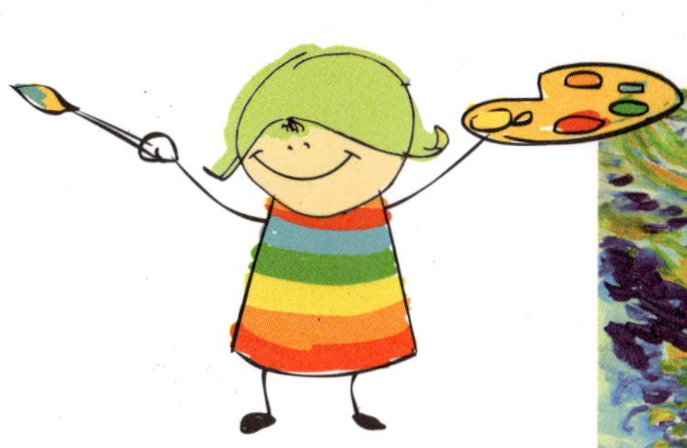

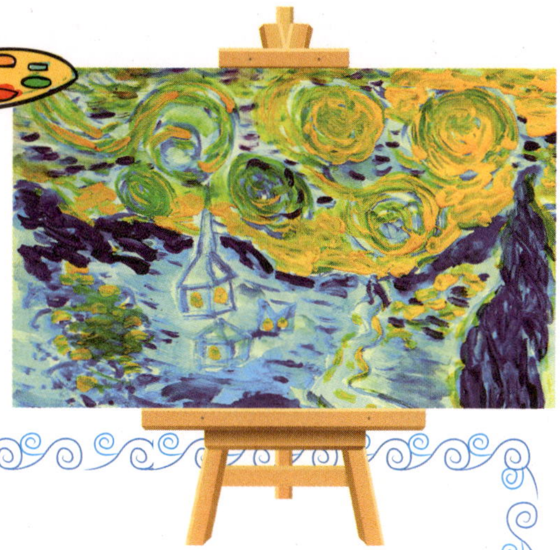

Teeny Tiny

It is time to draw some insects.
Colour them appropriately.

Draw the centre of the body and then add the wings and legs.

Word Expressions

Every word has a meaning. Write your favourite word in a way that the meaning is clear. Here are a few examples.

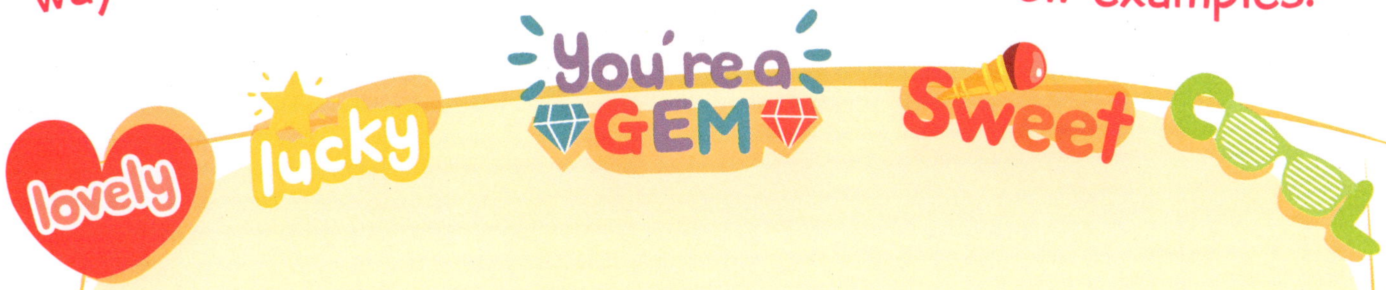

Dogs in Action

These dogs are doing various actions. Draw these animals and colour them black.

When an object is completely black, it is called a silhouette.

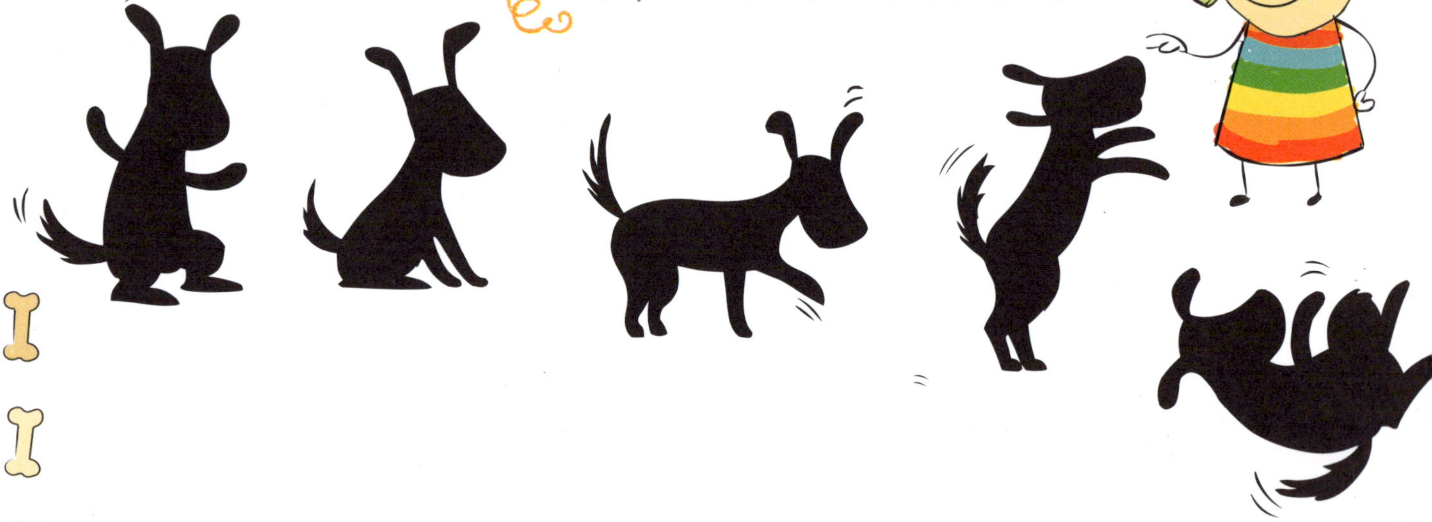

Cartoons Act

A lemon has been changed into a cartoon character. Draw this lemon with different expressions and doing different actions.

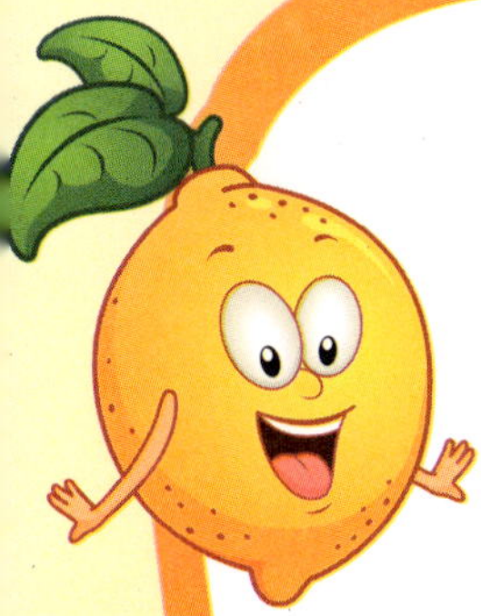

Action Figures

All these children are doing some actions. Practice drawing these human figures in the space given below.

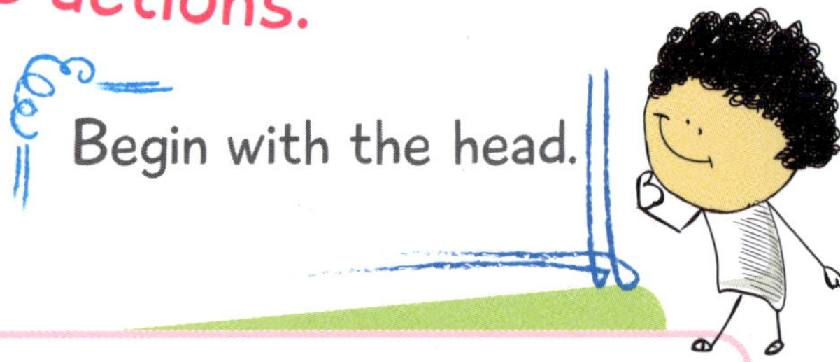

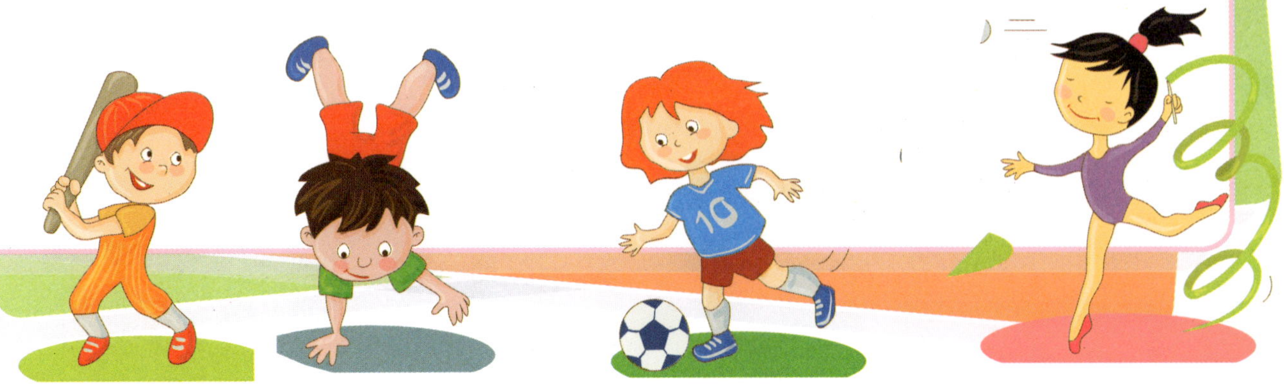

Draw and colour a sports tournament with lots of people in action in the space given below.

Market Chaos

A market is always full of people and activity. Complete this market scene in any manner you want.

Add more shops, people and animals to this picture.

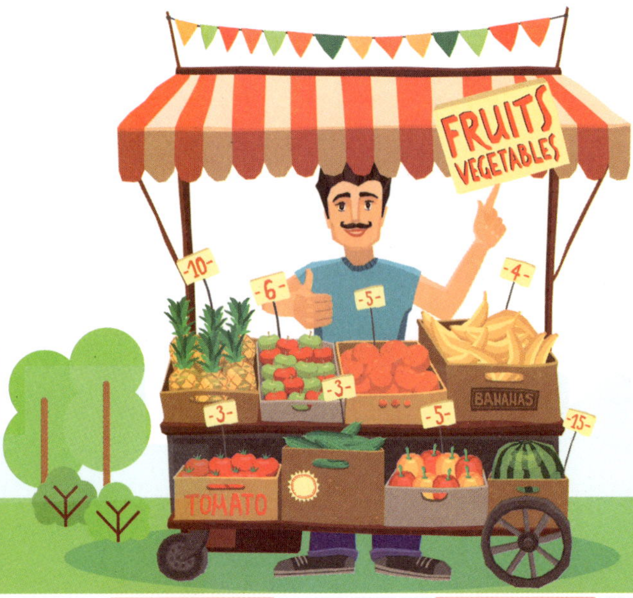

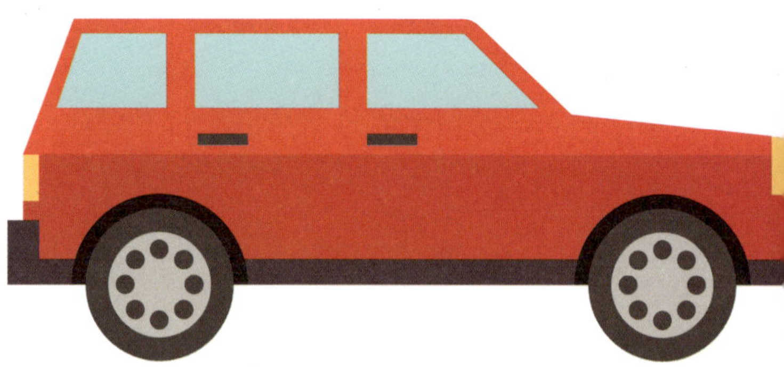

Tribal Masks

Colour the tribal masks using different vibrant colours.

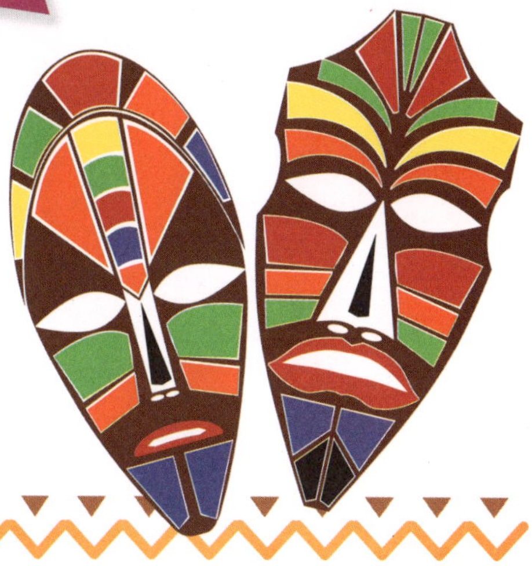

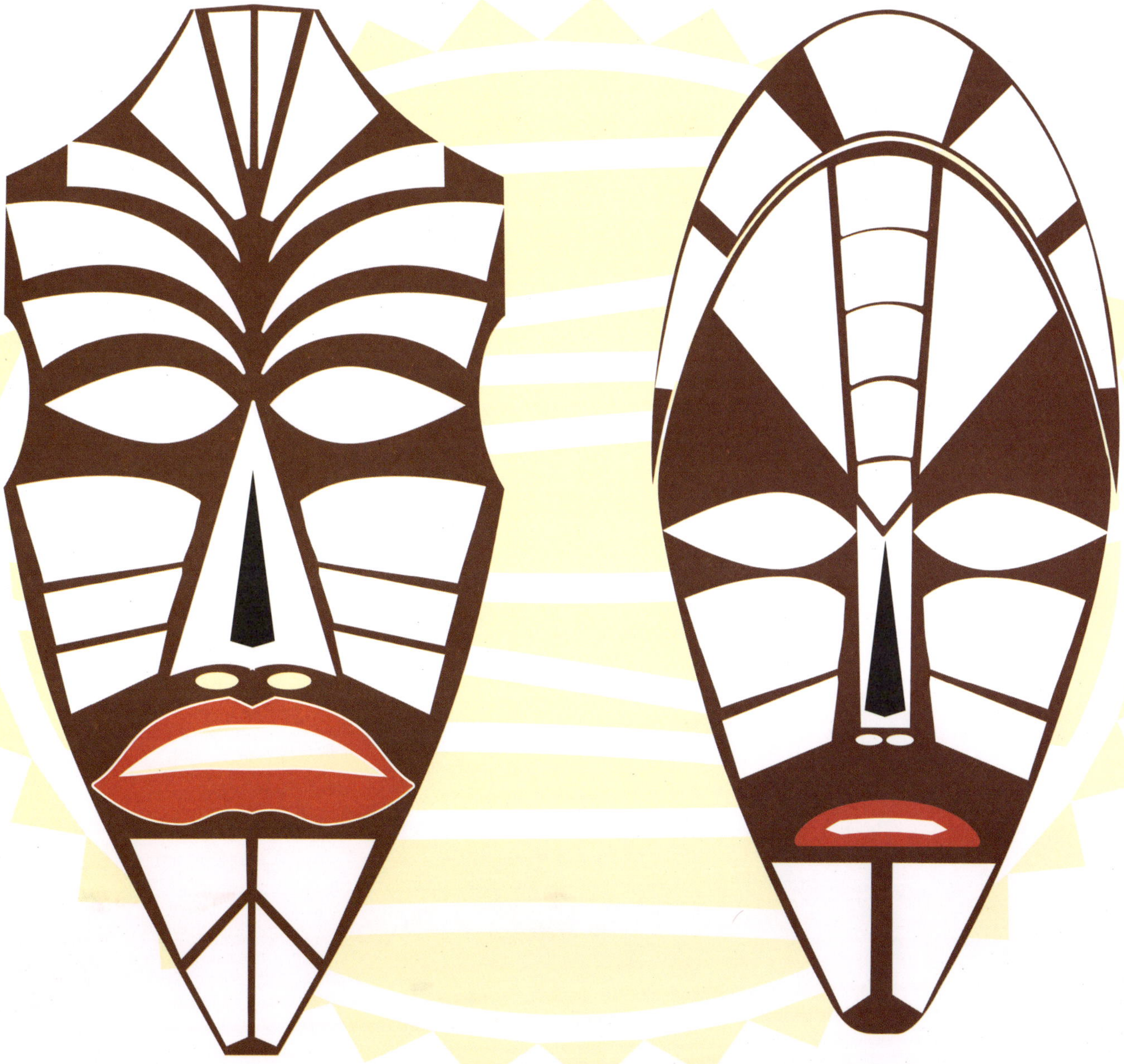

Tints and Shades

When white is added to a solid colour, it makes a tint.
When black is added to a solid colour, it makes a shade.
Colour these trees with the tints and shades of red.

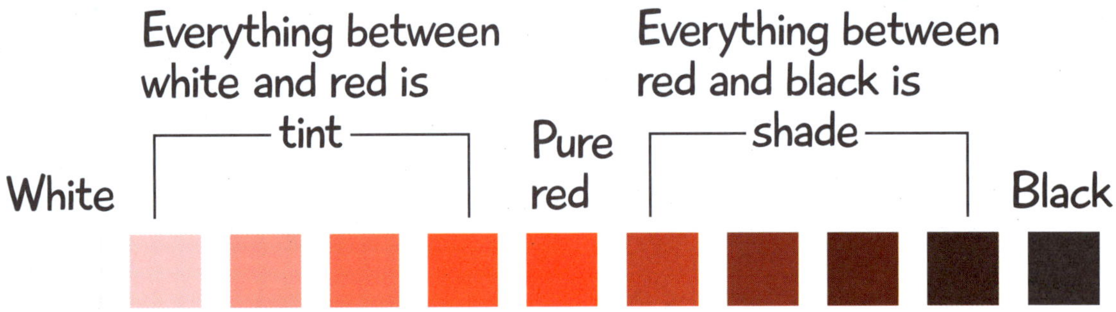

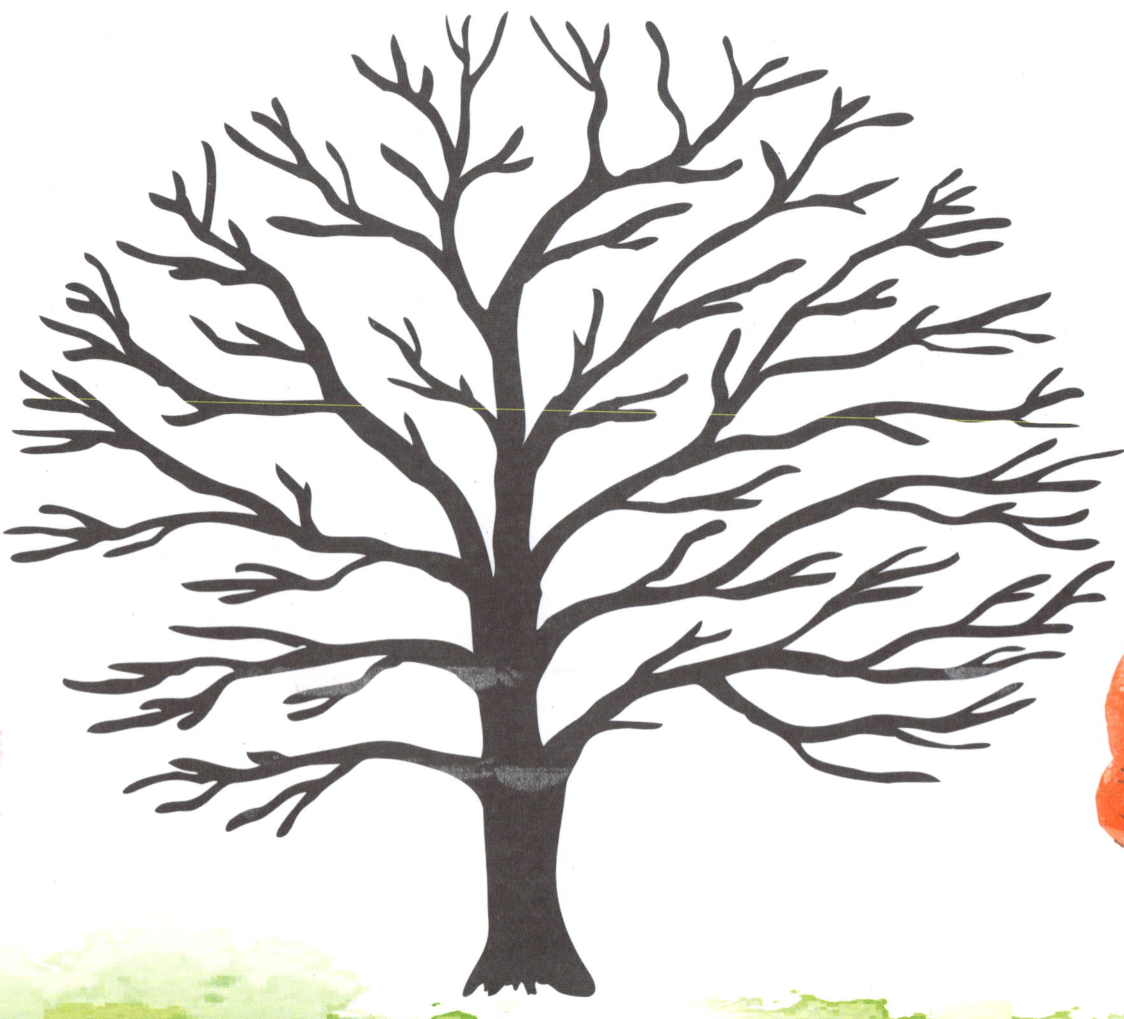

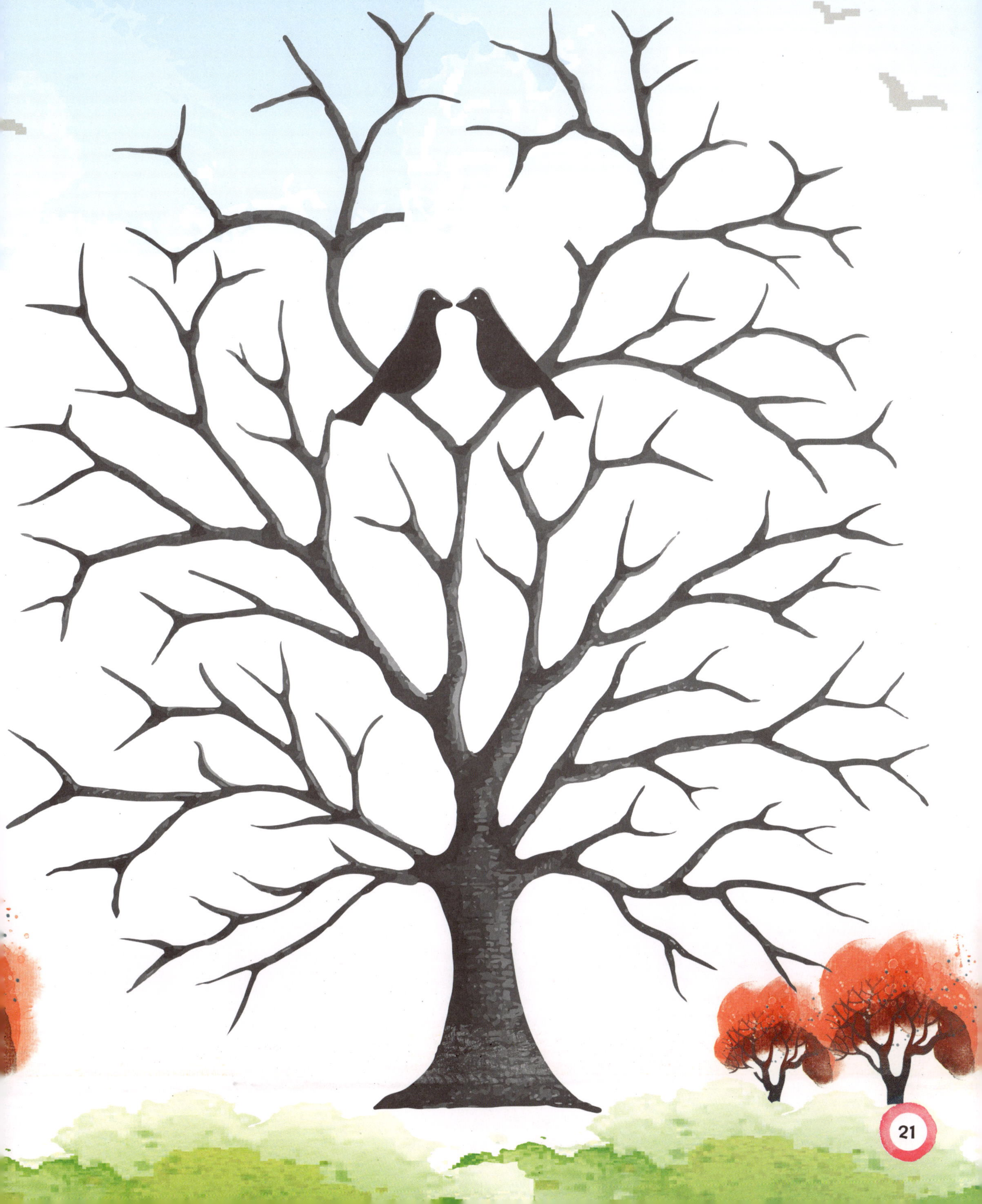

Reflections

You already know how to draw a skyline. Now, draw the reflection of this skyline.

Draw the reflection a little lighter than the skyline.

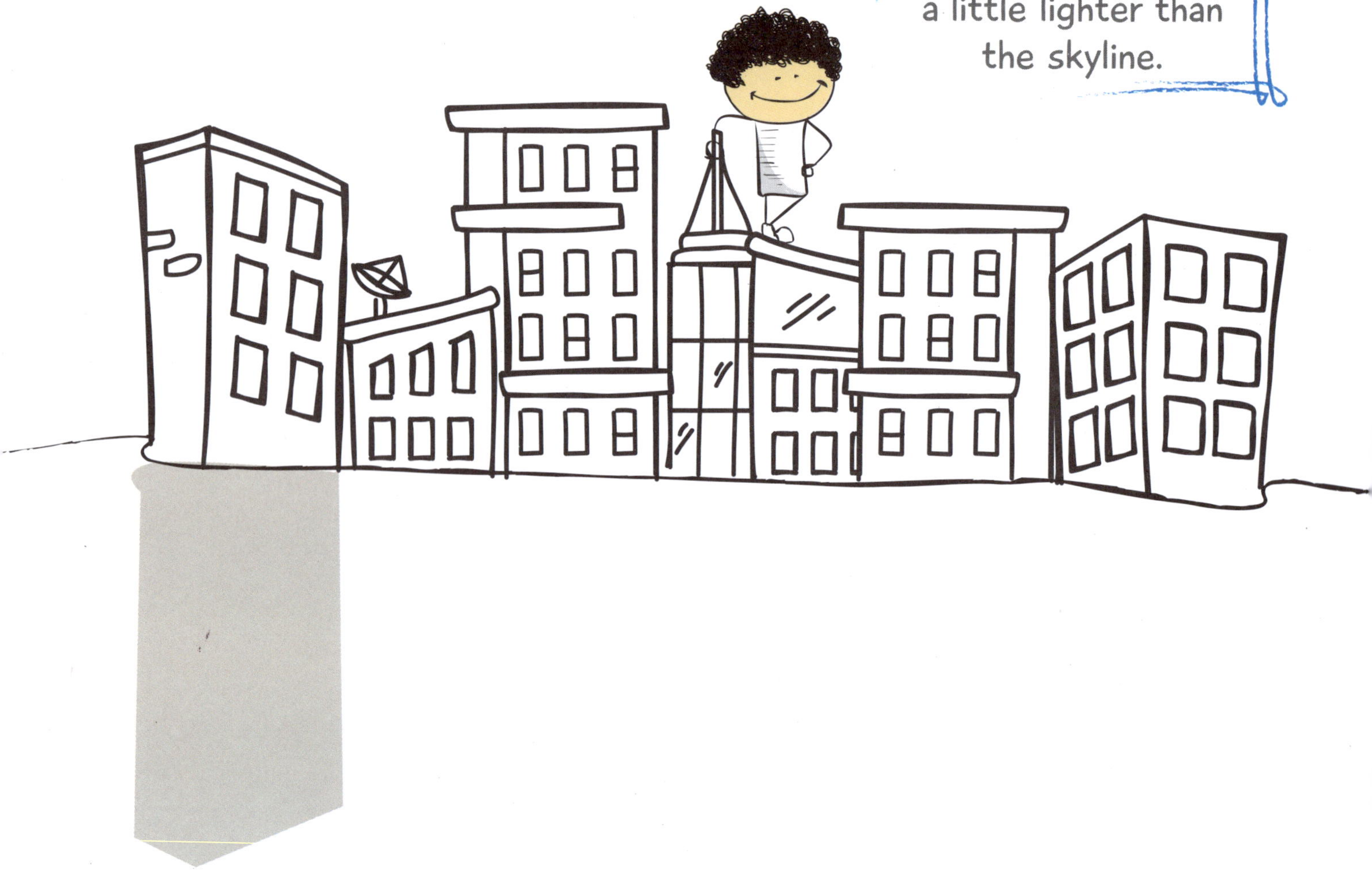

Perspective

Draw lines for the remaining shapes towards the dot in the centre of the page.

A drawing has one-point perspective when it contains only one vanishing point.

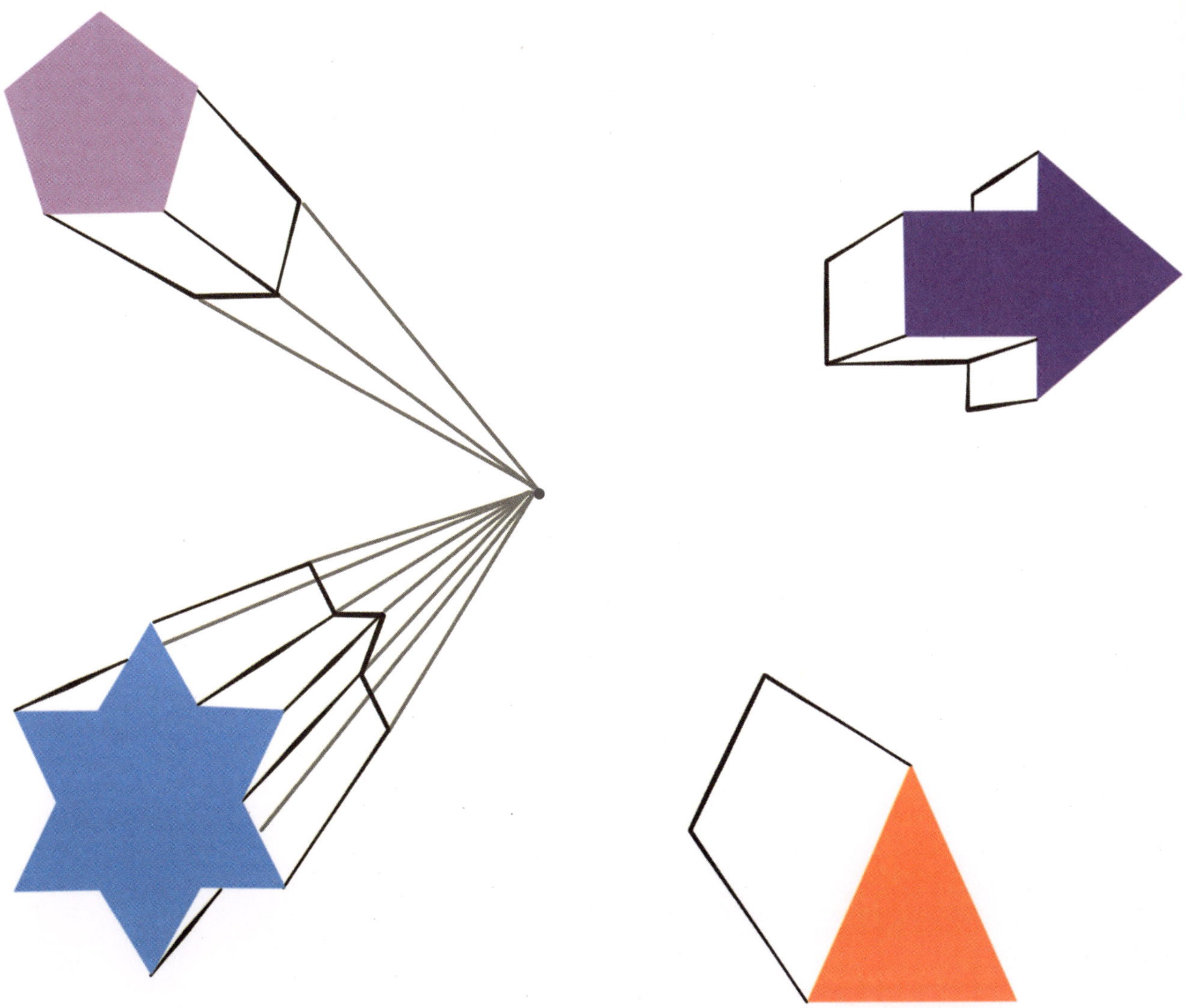

Optical Art

Make the same optical art on your own.
Use only pencil for this art.

Begin from the centre.

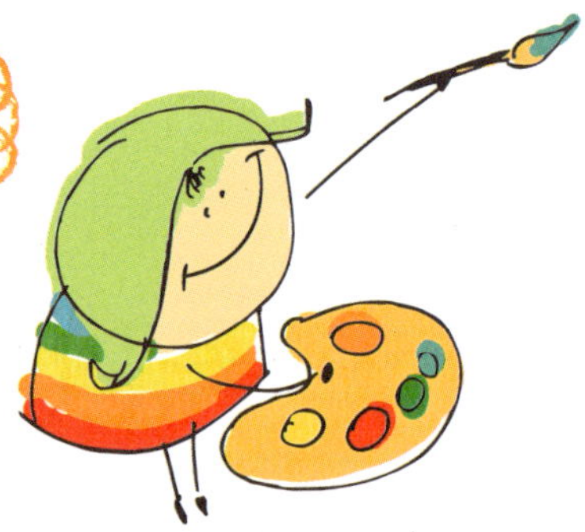

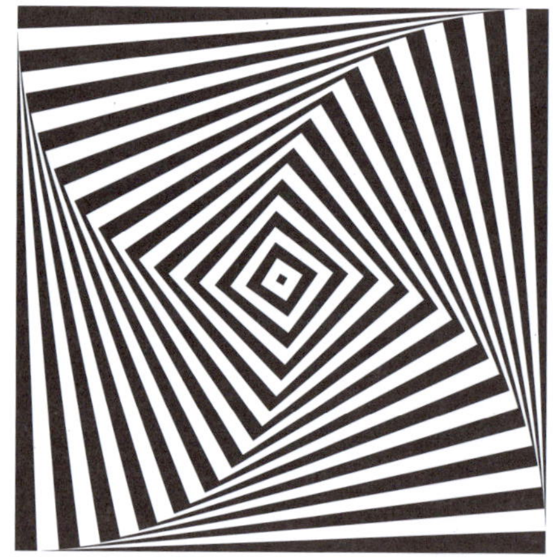

3D Illusions

Make squares one inside the other. Shade it with pencils to give it more depth.

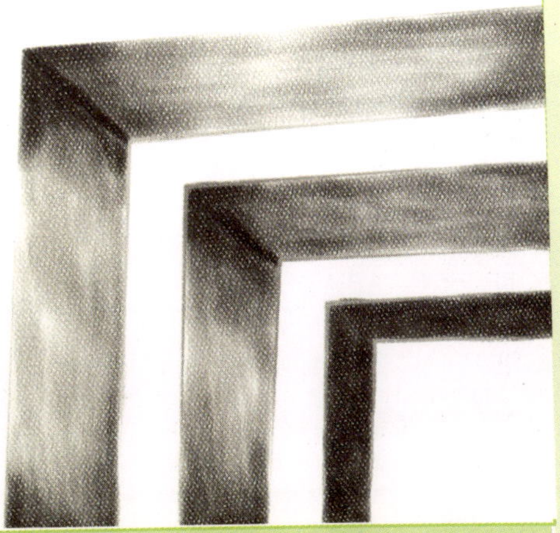

Coloured Water

Use water colours and a thin rounded brush to practice making flowers.

Mountains and Plains

Use blue and green to complete this painting of mountains and plains. Make it dark towards the edges.

Begin the painting from the top of the page so that your hand does not spoil the rest.

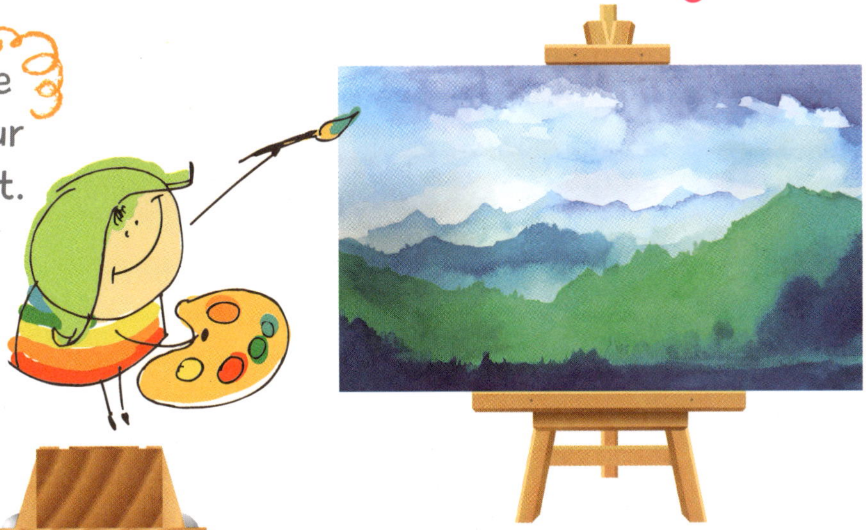

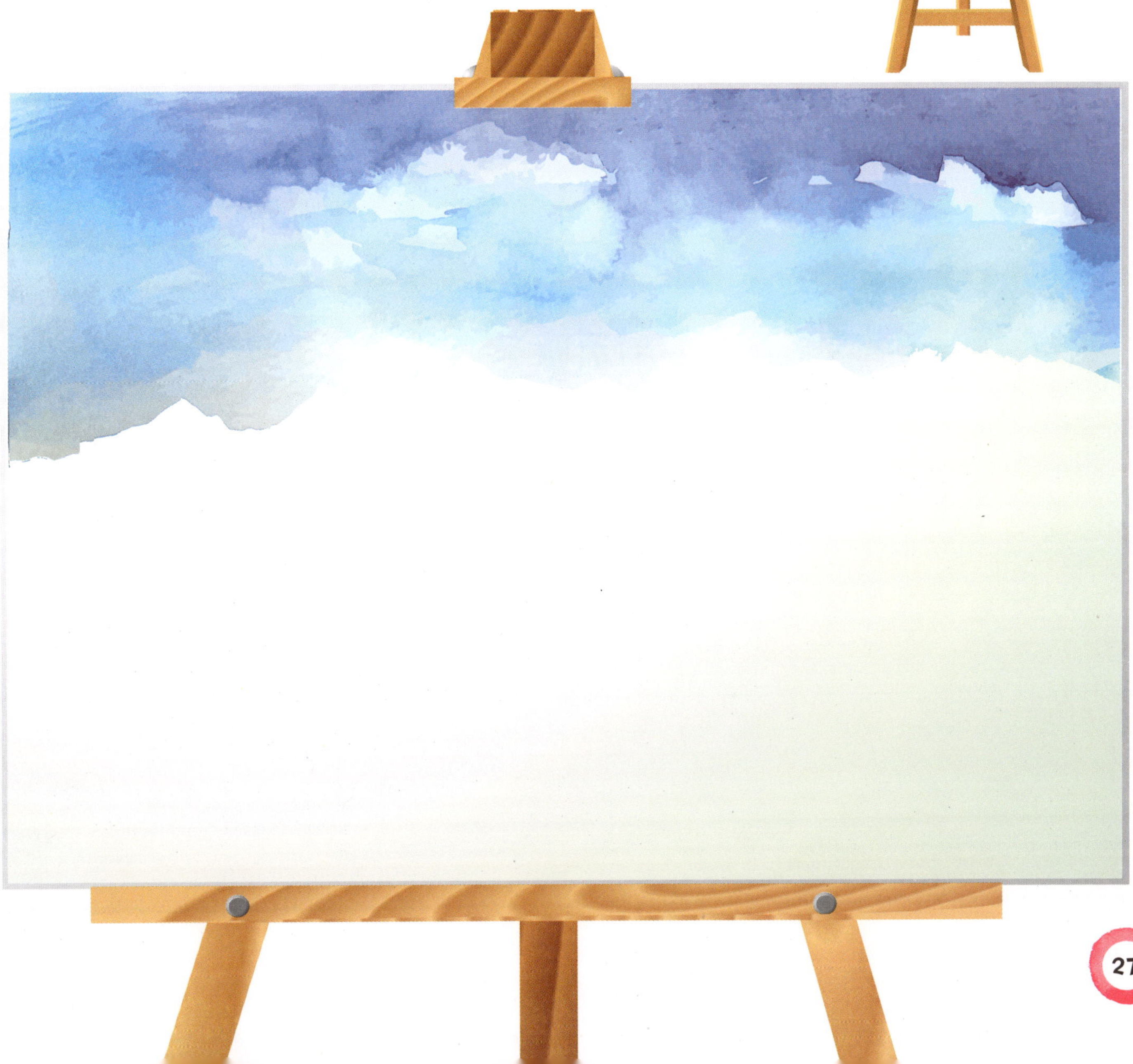

My Family

Can you draw your family? In the space given below, draw a family portrait and colour it.

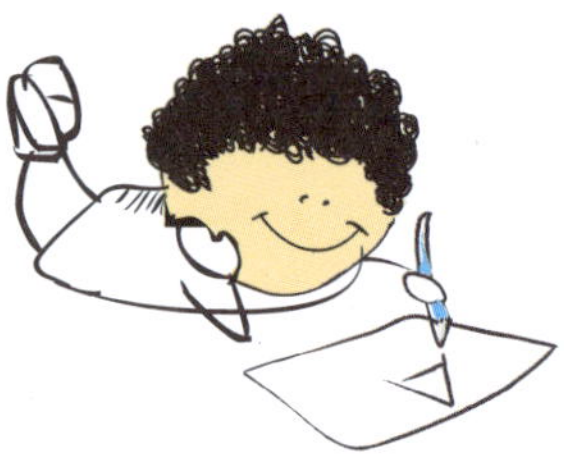

Make thin, black outlines to give your painting a finished look.

Complete the Pattern

Complete this design with what comes to you naturally in the form of different lines. Colour the design appropriately.

Keep lots of white spaces for a better effect. Use minimal colour.

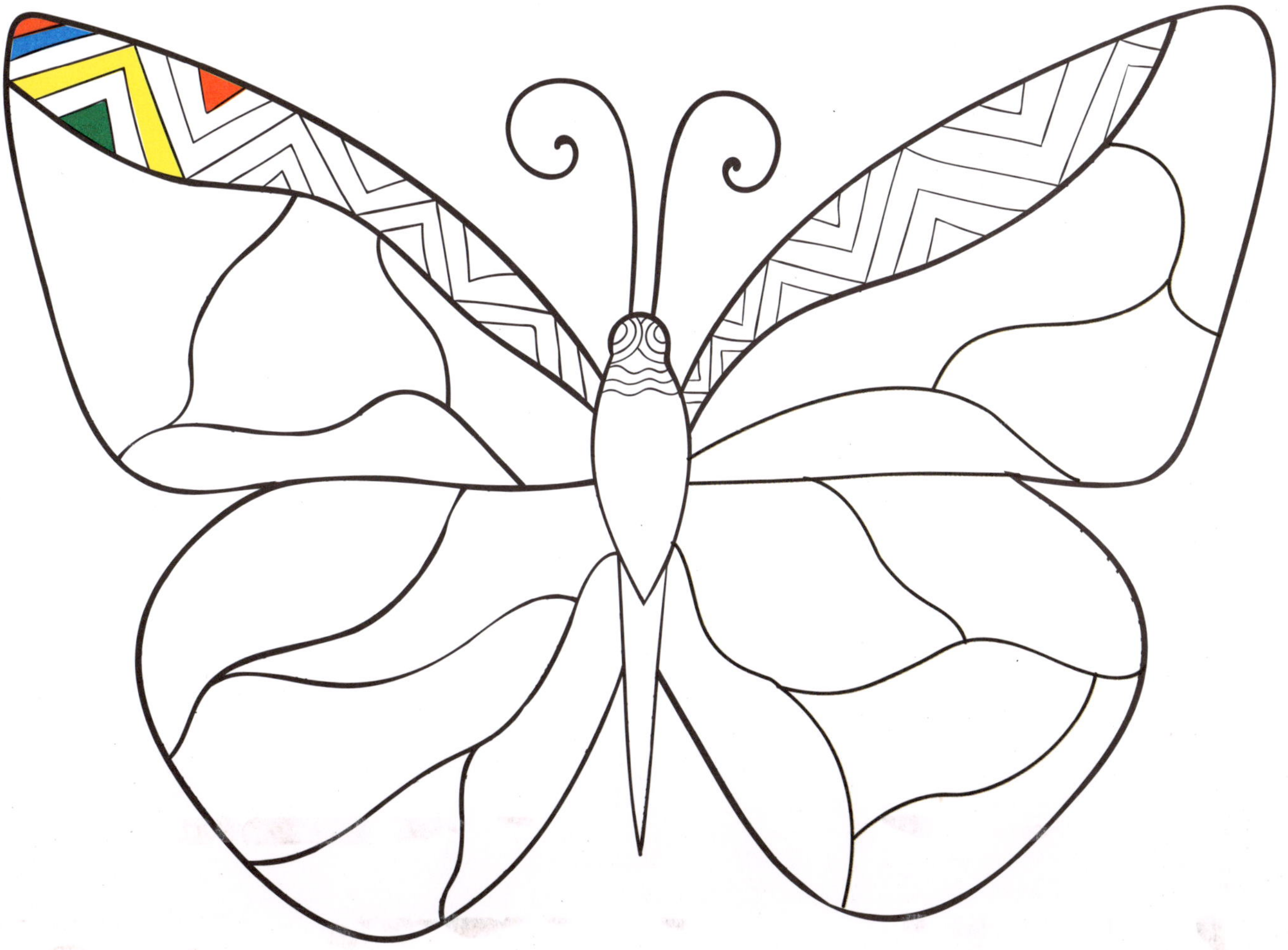

Stencil Art

Make a stencil painting in the box below.

You will need:

- Cut out of a star or any shape you like. (Needs to be smaller than the box below).
- Paints - water or poster
- An old toothbrush

Let us begin painting:

1. Place the cut out over the box on this page.
2. Dip a tooth brush in poster colours and run your thumb over it.
   It will create a spray like effect.
3. Spray around and over the cut out.
4. Once you are done, your stencil art is done!

Tie and Dye Effect

Let's try and make a Tie and Dye effect on paper!

You will need:
- Sketch pens

Bring out your sketch pens that represent the rainbow colours.

Let us begin sketching:

1. You will have to colour seven circles separately but at the same time mixed with the other.
2. So if you start the circle using light blue, ensure the next circle is in dark blue. Follow that with pink, red, brown, yellow and finish the final circle with green.
3. Your tie and dye effect sketch is ready. Take the difficulty a notch up by using water colours!

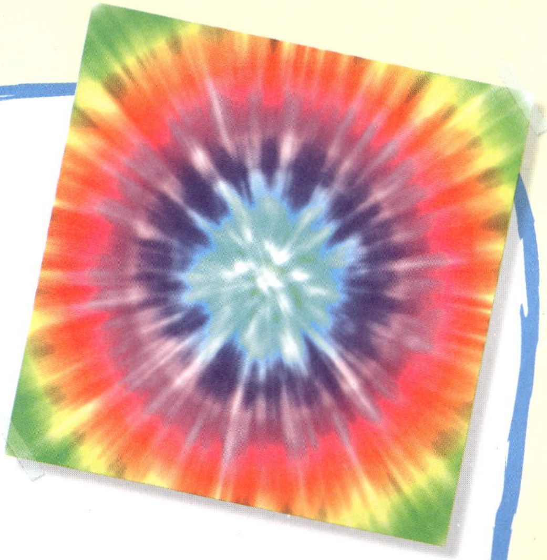

Creative Owl

Let us see how creative you are. Design the owl in any manner you want.

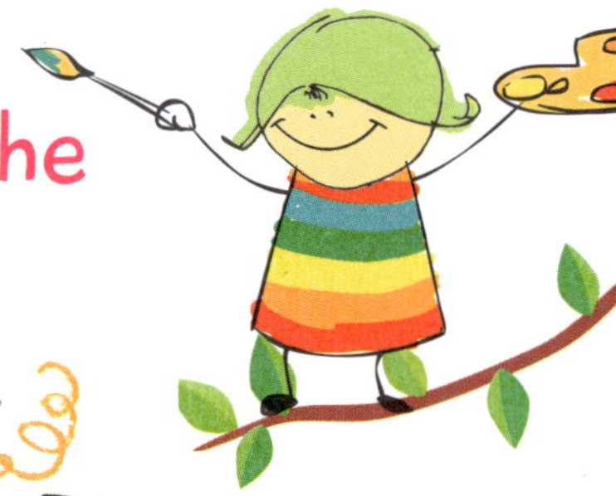

You can use colours as well.

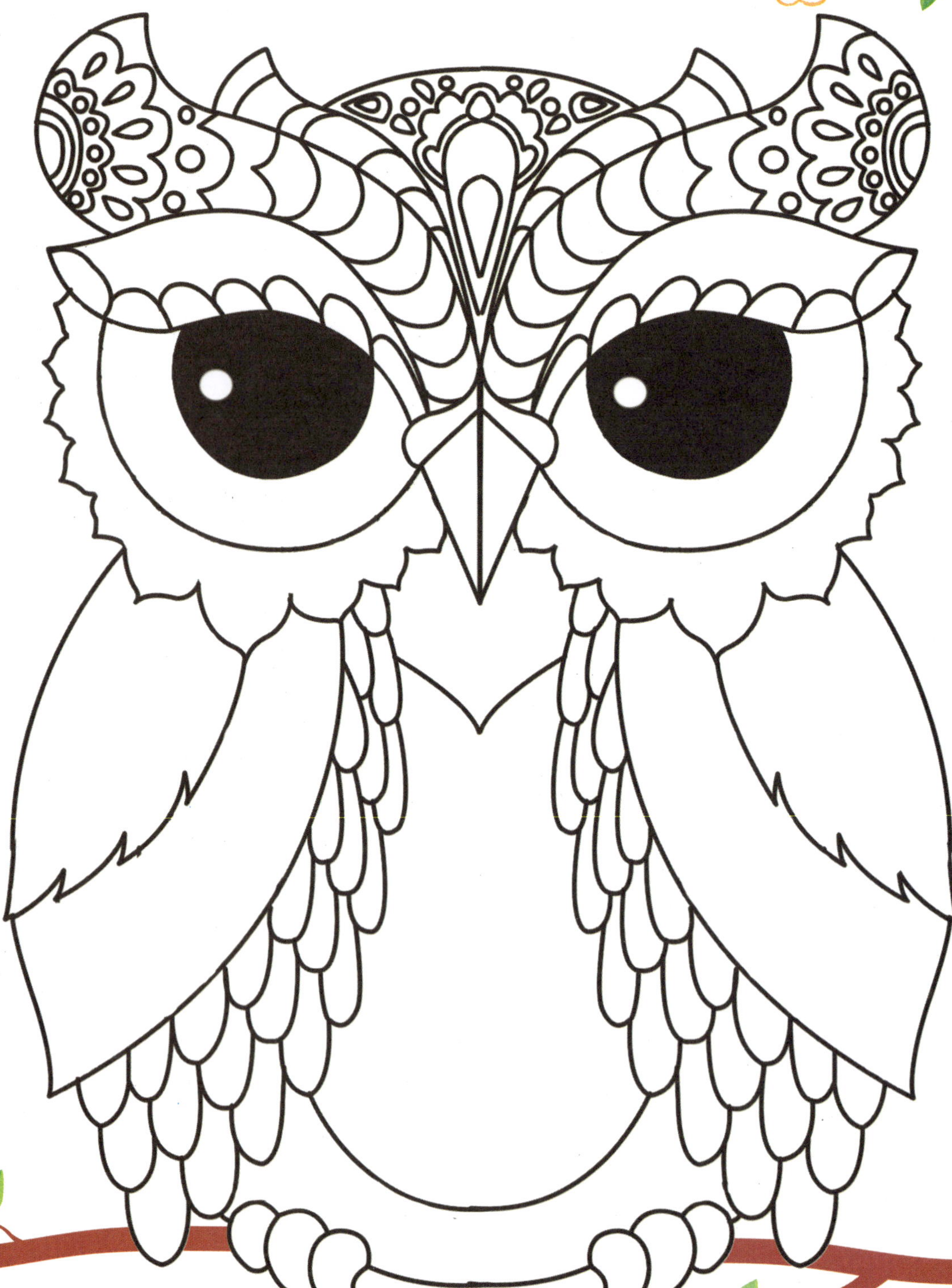